MY MASTER'S
VOICE

Hope for the Bereaved

Christine D. Murrow

Copyright © 2015 by Christine D. Murrow

My Master's Voice
Hope for the Bereaved
by Christine D. Murrow

Printed in the United States of America.

ISBN 9781498442541

All rights reserved solely by the author. The author guarantees all contents are original and do not infringe upon the legal rights of any other person or work. No part of this book may be reproduced in any form without the permission of the author. The views expressed in this book are not necessarily those of the publisher.

Unless otherwise indicated, Scripture quotations are taken from the New King James Version (NKJV). Copyright © 1979, 1980, 1982 by Thomas Nelson, Inc. Used by permission. All rights reserved.

www.xulonpress.com

SCRIPTURAL REFERENCE GUIDE

ALL FOR ME: Genesis 22:13

MY PRECIOUS LORD: Psalm 34:8, Matthew 14:35,36, Song of Solomon 2:1, Isaiah 61:3

MY MASTER'S VOICE: Zephaniah 3:17, Song of Solomon 6:3

GOD'S LOVE: Luke 19:40, Romans 8:22, Psalm 8:4-8

MY SOUL'S DESIRE: Ephesians 3:14-19, Psalm 51:11, Exodus 33:22, Psalm 4:1-8

BEAUTY FOR ASHES: Psalm 27:4

DEDICATION

I would like to dedicate this book of poems, my first literary work to my father, Richard J. Novy who has provided a lifetime of inspiration and laughter. He is a courageous man who has persevered in the face of adversity for more years than I can count, and it can truly be said of him that he has fought the good fight of faith.

I love you Dad. Thank you for being the wind in my sails more times than you will ever know and a living testimony of God's love. You will forever be the treasure in my heart.

Your Daughter,
Christine

FOREWORD

"The Spirit of the Lord GOD is upon Me, because the Lord has anointed Me to preach good tidings to the poor; He has sent Me to heal the brokenhearted, to proclaim liberty to the captives, and the opening of the prison to those who are bound; To proclaim the acceptable year of the Lord, and the day of vengeance of our God; To comfort all who mourn, to console those who mourn in Zion, to give them beauty for ashes, the oil of joy for mourning, the garment of praise for the spirit of heaviness; That they may be called trees of righteousness, the planting of the Lord, that He may be glorified."

Isaiah 61:1-3 (NKJV)

ALL FOR ME

Where are you my soul?
I seem to have lost you.
I'm here, beyond there
Waiting for thee.

One fleeting moment and all
Shall be lost,
But there in the thicket
Is caught the ram.

Just for me, and all for me
No thought for self,
You set me free.

Free to glory in laughter and peace.
A peace so sweet
My soul was afraid to reach
Out and taste.
But there You were!
Oh my soul, You are The Ram
Who gave Himself that I might live.

There was no fight
On that night.
The battle had been fought
and won
In the depth of your heart.

Once for me..
Once for all..
Love spilled out like oil
From an alabaster box.

Once for me..
Once for all..
Upon the ground atoned by love,
The greatest love of all..
The Ram, who came
and gave His life for me!

MY PRECIOUS LORD

My precious Lord,
My precious One..
It's all about You,
It's all about You.

You are the One
so holy and sweet.
Oh, taste and see
He's there before thee.

Reach out and touch
The hem so pure.
Receive your peace,
He's there for you.

Waiting, waiting..
For you to see
With eyes opened anew.

All in glory,
He stands before you
Waiting to be seen..
Waiting to be touched..
Waiting to be found..

Not hiding from you..
Nay, standing boldly before you.
Open your eyes and see..
Reach out your hand and touch..
Lift up your head and receive..

Sweet Lily of the Valley,
Sweet and Holy One!

Come with singing!
Come with joy!

FALL UPON THE GROUND BEFORE HIM.
COVER YOUR FACE AND WEEP.
FOR YOU HAVE SEEN THE FACE OF GOD
AND TOUCHED THE HAND
T'WAS SCARRED FOR YOU.

THE FULLNESS OF HIS GLORY
OVER-SHADOWED YOU
AND TOOK YOU IN.
OH, ABBA FATHER,
WHERE HAVE YOU BEEN?
ALL THE WHILE, CHILD
BEFORE YOU.

I ONCE WAS BLIND,
BUT NOW I SEE
THY BEAUTY FOR ASHES
THOU GAVE TO ME.

AMEN

MY MASTER'S VOICE

My heart is full, I know not why.
Could it be that My Savior sings
over me?
The sweet soft melody, the
soft resound
Of I once was lost but now am found.

Believe me forever,
"Hear me", I cry;
The voice of my Master
Drifts from on high,
Follows me 'ere I go.

Loves me,
Lifts me,
Calls out my name.

Wooing, beckoning, drawing me near
Into His bosom where I lie
down to rest
Apart from the world
Safe in His care.
His watch is over me.
His love surrounds me.

What tender bliss,
One sweet kiss.
I'm yours at last
And You are mine.

GOD'S PERFECT LOVE

One day at a time..
Moment by moment..
Your love unfolds
Before my eyes.

There you are my Sweet One
In the sparkle of sky between
The leaves..
Again in the babble of the
Glistening creek..

Beyond every mountain..
You adorn every stream..
The rocks cry out!
Your creation groans,
"Master, come near me."

I'm ruined by love.

You melt the mountains..
You dry up the streams..
And lay them at my feet
As the measure of Your love for me.

Who am I that I should deserve
The universe and every curve
Of nature beyond?

What is this that you say?
I am the bride, Your heart's delight!

You counted me worthy
And drew Your last breath
That I might be with You.

Selah

MY SOUL'S DESIRE

My sweet, sweet love..
My soul's only desire..
I lie at Your feet
And count the hours
'til You come for me.

To fathom Your love
Is to measure the mountains,
The height and breadth of the sky,
The depth of the seas,
The sand of its shores,
Magnitude and multitude,
Mountains and monuments.

Greatness, greatness!
You cannot be contained nor
measured, nor explained.

"You are; You are,"
Out of the heart the mouth speaks!

Breathe on me Your Holy
Precious Spirit.
Renew me and strengthen
my wings that I might
fly to Your very throne!

Cast me not from Thy presence,
But hide me in the cleft of the rock.
Preserve me until the hour of
Redemption.
In the shelter of Your wings
I am safe.

BEAUTY FOR ASHES

My Lord, my Lord
Thou hast beauty beyond measure
Your face I see
And delight in Thee.
Forever and ever I will be
Thy daughter and first love.

Kindle not the fire of enmity in me
But let love and beauty for ashes be.
Find not fault in my doings
For it is mercy and patience I ask
of Thee.

Lean down from Heaven and
kiss my face
You surely love this human race.

> BE STILL MY HEART WHEN AT
> DEATH'S DOOR
> FOR YOU SHALL LIVE FOREVERMORE.

www.ingramcontent.com/pod-product-compliance
Lightning Source LLC
LaVergne TN
LVHW041554060526
838200LV00037B/1281